GUIDE

MW01114108

Christian Education

Planning for Lifelong Faith Formation

Diana L. Hynson
General Board of Discipleship

CHRISTIAN EDUCATION

Copyright © 2012 by Cokesbury

This book is printed on acid-free paper.

ISBN 978-1-426-73642-1

Some paragraph numbers for and language in the Book of Discipline *may have changed in the 2012 revision, which was published after these Guidelines were printed. We regret any inconvenience.*

MANUFACTURED IN THE UNITED STATES OF AMERICA

Contents

Called to a Ministry of Faithfulness and Vitality

You are so important to the life of the Christian church! You have consented to join with other people of faith who, through the millennia, have sustained the church by extending God's love to others. You have been called and have committed your unique passions, gifts, and abilities to a position of leadership. This Guideline will help you understand the basic elements of that ministry within your own church and within The United Methodist Church.

Leadership in Vital Ministry

Each person is called to ministry by virtue of his or her baptism, and that ministry takes place in all aspects of daily life, both in and outside of the church. Your leadership role requires that you will be a faithful participant in the **mission of the church**, which is to partner with God to **make disciples of Jesus Christ for the transformation of the world**. You will not only engage in your area of ministry, but will also work to empower others to be in ministry as well. The vitality of your church, and the Church as a whole, depends upon the faith, abilities, and actions of all who work together for the glory of God.

Clearly then, as a pastoral leader or leader among the laity, your ministry is not just a "job," but a spiritual endeavor. You are a spiritual leader now, and others will look to you for spiritual leadership. What does this mean?

All persons who follow Jesus are called to grow spiritually through the practice of various Christian habits (or "means of grace") such as prayer, Bible study, private and corporate worship, acts of service, Christian conferencing, and so on. Jesus taught his disciples practices of spiritual growth and leadership that you will model as you guide others. As members of the congregation grow through the means of grace, they will assume their own role in ministry and help others in the same way. This is the cycle of disciple making.

The Church's Vision

While there is one mission—to make disciples of Jesus Christ—the portrait of a successful mission will differ from one congregation to the next. One of your roles is to listen deeply for the guidance and call of God in your own context. In your church, neighborhood, or greater community, what are the greatest needs? How is God calling your congregation to be in a ministry of service and witness where they are? What does vital ministry look like in the life of your congregation and its neighbors? What are the characteristics, traits, and actions that identify a person as a faithful disciple in your context?

This portrait, or vision, is formed when you and the other leaders discern together how your gifts from God come together to fulfill the will of God.

Assessing Your Efforts

We are generally good at deciding what to do, but we sometimes skip the more important first question of what we want to accomplish. Knowing your task (the mission of disciple making) and knowing what results you want (the vision of your church) are the first two steps in a vital ministry. The third step is in knowing how you will assess or measure the results of what you do and who you are (and become) because of what you do. Those measures relate directly to mission and vision, and they are more than just numbers.

One of your leadership tasks will be to take a hard look, with your team, at all the things your ministry area does or plans to do. No doubt they are good and worthy activities; the question is, *"Do these activities and experiences lead people into a mature relationship with God and a life of deeper discipleship?"* That is the business of the church, and the church needs to do what only the church can do. You may need to eliminate or alter some of what you do if it does not measure up to the standard of faithful disciple making. It will be up to your ministry team to establish the specific standards against which you compare all that you do and hope to do. (This Guideline includes further help in establishing goals, strategies, and measures for this area of ministry.)

The Mission of The United Methodist Church

Each local church is unique, yet it is a part of a *connection,* a living organism of the body of Christ. Being a connectional Church means in part that all United Methodist churches are interrelated through the structure and organization of districts, conferences, and jurisdictions in the larger "family" of the denomination. *The Book of Discipline of The United Methodist Church* describes, among other things, the ministry of all United Methodist Christians, the essence of servant ministry and leadership, how to organize and accomplish that ministry, and how our connectional structure works (see especially ¶¶126–138).

Our Church extends way beyond your doorstep; it is a global Church with both local and international presence. You are not alone. The resources of the entire denomination are intended to assist you in ministry. With this help and the partnership of God and one another, the mission continues. You are an integral part of God's church and God's plan!

(For help in addition to this Guideline and the *Book of Discipline*, see "Resources" at the end of your Guideline, www.umc.org, and the other websites listed on the inside back cover.)

The Purpose of Christian Education

education is as natural a part of life as breathing. From the day of our birth (or even before) we are learning. As babies we explore our fingers and toes, then progress to basic trust. We are taught our ABCs and how to tie our shoes. We discover what tastes good and what tastes yucky. And we go on from there. Life is about learning, growing, adapting, and learning some more. It follows, then, that we must be taught the ABCs of our faith, faith tradition, and Church. That, simply stated, is the role of the ministry of Christian education, though there is more.

Form, Inform, and Transform

All of life's experiences serve to shape us into the people we are and will become. The baby who learns basic trust is formed in a very different way from the child who doesn't. The child who easily learns life's early tasks has a distinctly different path than the child who struggles to grasp those lessons. We are formed from day one and never stop, because whatever happens (or doesn't happen) has an effect on our character, values, decisions, and behavior. As Christians and as teachers or leaders in Christian education, we carry tremendous responsibility and opportunity to forge values and behaviors that are biblically based, theologically sound, and faithfully lived out. We endeavor to form people as Christian disciples for the transformation of the world.

The ministry of Christian education and formation is a teaching ministry. Content—facts, dates, explanations, maps, meanings—is central to this ministry. It's important to know the who's who, the what and when, the how and why of our faith as it is recorded in the Bible and beyond. It is hard to live by the words and life of Christ if we have not read or learned them.

Information, no matter how crucial, cannot carry all the weight of Christian education ministry. *Knowing about* God, Jesus Christ, the Holy Spirit, and the acts of the Apostles is just a part of the whole. *Knowing* God through Christ, with the help of the Holy Spirit and the saints of the church, is what takes us from being biblically literate students to being mature disciples who actively love God and neighbor. Knowing *and* experiencing lead to transformation.

While it is true that all of life shapes us, we are not necessarily formed with the values and principles of faith that God would desire. As we learn and develop in God's grace, we are necessarily changed—transformed—as we grow into the likeness of Christ. Becoming Christ-like is the ultimate goal for the well formed, informed, and transformed Christian disciple.

Bible Study Is a Spiritual Discipline

Practices that help to mold Christian character and to cultivate a relationship with God are referred to as *spiritual disciplines, ordinances*, or *means of grace*. John Wesley, the founder of Methodism, mentions several means of grace in his rules for the covenantal groups he organized: the public worship of God; the ministry of the Word, either read or expounded; the Supper of the Lord; family and private prayer; searching the Scriptures; and fasting or abstinence. (See "The Nature, Design, and General Rules of Our United Societies," ¶104, in *The Book of Discipline of The United Methodist Church*.)

Wesley believed that these ordinances together (along with others that involve service and peace with justice) would give the Christian—particularly the novice Christian—structure, focus, and practice in the things that cultivate the faithful and spiritual life. Each is valuable in its own right, but together, they help the Christian disciple to develop a well-rounded relationship to God through Christ that cares both for the soul of the believer and that believer's participation in church and society.

As a leader or teacher in Christian education, you will want to instill in your teachers and students the importance of being well-steeped in the Scriptures. The participants in your classes and groups, particularly children and youth, will look to the leader as the "resident expert" who can answer questions and help them make meaning of the Word of God. While none of you is expected to be the infallible Bible scholar, being well-acquainted and well-studied with the Scriptures will offer a needed role model for this important discipline.

A Biblical/Theological Foundation

For John Wesley, there was no holiness except for social holiness, which means that one must learn the Scriptures—what they say and what they mean—and then act on those learned precepts. One learned and cultivated his or her own relationship with God, and then went out to love and serve God and neighbor. Brother Charles Wesley expressed this in one of his many hymns that set the Wesley's theology to music: to "Unite those two so long disjoin'd: / Knowledge and vital piety" (*The Poetical Works of John and Charles Wesley*, Vol VI, London, 1870; Hymn 40; to be used at the opening of a school in Kingswood).

THE QUADRILATERAL

One's "vital piety" was fueled by knowledge; in this case, knowledge of the Scriptures. A distinctive gift of the Wesleys was the structure of making meaning through what we call the Wesleyan Quadrilateral: Scripture, tradition, reason, and experience. Of these four filters, Scripture is primary. In discerning the meaning of a portion of Scripture, making a decision, devising a course of action, or focusing one's values, the first step is to examine the Bible. Each text can be weighed against other texts so that nothing is simply pulled out of context. Obviously, we can't discern or measure our actions and choices through the lens of Scripture if we are not familiar with the Scriptures, which makes the study of Scripture so important in cultivating a life of faith.

Tradition refers to the long history of God's action in the communities of faith and through the history of the church. Reason is that God-given gift of thinking critically and working out decisions thoughtfully. Experience refers not only to one's own experience, but also to the witness of others' experiences. These four together provide a faithful and thoughtful check and balance system for weighing, judging, and making decisions. Scripture is foremost in this quadrilateral; another compelling reason for a thorough, lifelong system of Christian education and formation.

BIBLICAL FOUNDATION
While the Wesleys have given us a valuable legacy, faith education is first mandated in Scripture. The Proverbs, for example, have numerous short, pithy sayings praising the virtue of wisdom and learning, starting with the first one. "The fear of the LORD" (meaning the righteous life) "is the beginning of knowledge; / fools despise wisdom and instruction" (1:7). Wisdom is to be valued, but not simply as an end in itself. "Keep hold of instruction; do not let go / guard her, for she is your life" (4:13; see also Proverbs 2–3).

We would expect the Wisdom literature (Proverbs, Job, and Ecclesiastes) to champion learning, but this mandate is found elsewhere. Deuteronomy 6, for example, is a part of the address of Moses to the people of Israel who have just received what we know as the Ten Commandments. This lengthy discourse by Moses, giving over to the people what God has commanded him, is not intended simply for the immediate hearers, but for their children and their children's children. These statutes and ordinances have a purpose. "You must diligently keep the commandments of the LORD your God, and his decrees, and his statutes, that he has commanded you. Do what is right and good in the sight of the LORD, so that it may go well with you, and so that you may go in and occupy the good land that the LORD swore to our ancestors to give you.... When your children ask you in the time to come, 'What is the meaning of the decrees and the statutes and the ordinances that the LORD our God has commanded you?' then you shall say to your children, 'We were Pharaoh's slaves in Egypt, but the Lord brought us out of Egypt with a mighty hand'" (6:17-21). God's instruction is practical (the statutes and commandments that describe the righteous life); life-long (telling your children in time to come); and life-giving (the LORD brought us out...with a mighty hand).

The Old Testament foundation is reinforced in the New Testament. The most prevalent witness is Jesus—the master teacher and storyteller. The ultimate point of most of the parables is to draw out a portrait of the kingdom of God—what it looks like and what is the character of those who will inherit the Kingdom. Yet many, if not all, of the parables are open-ended, leaving room for the hearer to work with them in their own minds, drawing out the lessons meant just for them. Lessons we work out for ourselves are the ones longest remembered.

We are forgetful, though, and Jesus prepared his initial disciples and us for that eventuality. In his last long conversation with his intimates, Jesus promised them support: "I will ask the Father, and he will give you another Advocate, to be with you forever.... The Advocate, the Holy Spirit, whom the Father will send in my name, will teach you everything, and remind you of all that I have said to you" (John 14:15, 26). The entire Godhead— Father/Creator, Son, and Holy Spirit—are involved in providing us with wisdom and knowledge and in empowering us to teach and nurture others in the faith, so that we may have life.

CHRISTIAN EDUCATION IN VITAL MINISTRY

The term *Christian education* has unfortunately lost a bit of luster over the years because it apparently conjures up an image of an old, not-so-effective classroom model of delivering content. Content is important, but it may be more accurate to think in terms of Christian education and formation. If Christian education is life-giving—vital—we must necessarily include formation.

Much has been said about vital ministry, often referring to the lifespan or health of the congregation as a whole. Christian education and formation is intimately involved in the vitality of a congregation, for it transmits the faith, tells our corporate Story, gives us insight into how to live and what to value, and transforms us into the image of God. When Jesus said to his followers, "Do not be afraid, little flock, for it is your Father's good pleasure to give you the kingdom" (Luke 12:32), he was telling them in the most caring and compassionate way that God wants abundance and wholeness for all of us. Christian education and transformation is one ministry that helps us understand the Kingdom that God wants us to inherit and how to live in it. As beneficiaries of that grace, we share it with others.

Getting Started

You have consented to assume a leadership position, perhaps with great eagerness; perhaps with some trepidation. Now it is time to get started. This Guideline will give you basic information about the ministry, what needs to be done or considered, and how to dig in. **Most of the topics here have links or books to more information.** Be sure to check the Resources section.

What Are My Responsibilities?

Your responsibilities will probably include planning and visioning, working with teachers, handling administrative details, and more. Clearly the extent of your particular work depends on what position you have assumed. While these teams or positions will be defined and identified by local churches in their own way, this Guideline will be helpful for you if you are
- the chairperson of the Christian education team
- the church school superintendent
- the leader of small group ministry (there is a separate Guideline for you)
- a leader for a specific age-level (there are separate Guidelines for you)
- a staff member related to Christian education

If you are in a small membership church, you may fill all of these functions as well as teaching. If your church has some or all of these positions you automatically have ministry partners and you will want to clarify with them how these responsibilities are divided and handled.

This Guideline is written mainly to the role of the Education chairperson, because that position has the broadest range of responsibilities. This Guideline is *suggestive*. You will not be expected to do everything that is covered here, but the more you know about what could be done, the more complete your ministry of education will be.

JOB DESCRIPTIONS
A job description, particularly in a small membership church, may seem a bit formal or unnecessary, but it is important for several reasons.
- You need clarity about what you are supposed to do.
- If those expectations are in writing, there is no confusion.
- You need clear expectations in order to evaluate the education/formation ministry and also your performance.
- When everyone has the same understanding, you lessen the risk of turf arguments or competition, details "falling through the cracks," fuzzy goals, disappointments, and unexpected problems. You increase the pos-

sibilities of effective and efficient leadership, ministry satisfaction, and problem solving.

TIP: *If you have not received a list of responsibilities, ask for one. If there isn't one, work out your own, in consultation with the church council.*

If you don't have any written expectations for your area of ministry, seriously consider working that out yourself. Read this Guideline and whatever other resources help you, then "get your feet wet." Ask your predecessor how he or she organized, administered, and led. (Don't just copy without being sure that is the best way to go.) Live with this ministry for a while, work with your team, and then codify and record the responsibilities.

EDUCATION/ FORMATION RESPONSIBILITIES

You have been tapped as a leader, so you need to lead, not just to maintain the status quo. Leaders will analyze what is happening currently, assess what is missing or needed, and look ahead. Ideally, you will both manage the ministry that is and anticipate the ministry that could be. As you anticipate that future, you can plan strategies and goals that will get you there.

This list will be tailored by your church; but you may expect to
- lead meetings of your team to plan and assess what is happening and what needs to happen
- lead efforts to create education and formation settings for persons of all ages
- recruit teachers
- lead training or find outside help
- nurture teachers so that they are equipped personally and spiritually to continue in their class or group
- arrange for substitute teachers or group leaders
- explore curriculum options; order curriculum and supplies
- work out and manage a budget
- identify, teach, and monitor the necessary policies, procedures, and Safe Sanctuaries® guidelines, including arrangements for background checks
- communicate, through the church council or other means, the accomplishments, opportunities, and needs of this ministry
- evaluate the overall ministry and the various events, classes, and teachers

As a designated leader, you are also a member of the church council, representing the broad area of Christian education and formation. Ideally, the goals and strategies of the education/formation ministry support, and are supported by, the other ministry areas.

Ministry Partners

You are not and should not be alone in your Christian education leadership, even if you are in a very small membership church. No matter if you are the chairperson, Sunday school superintendant, and only teacher all rolled into one, you are not, and should not be alone. One person should not be guiding the entire course of Christian education or making unilateral decisions about curriculum, events, or other programming.

PRIMARY PARTNERS

Teachers and group leaders: In any size congregation, you will want a good relationship with the people who are involved directly with students and group members. (More on this in the next section.)

Age-level leaders: Mid-size or larger congregations may divide responsibility for Christian education and formation according to age-level. This could include a children's coordinator, youth leader, nursery workers, and so on. While each age-specific leader is responsible for that age group, a vital ministry will coordinate the flow of learning and experiences so that children and youth can progress as smoothly as possible from one level to the next. (This is seldom smooth, though, as people come and go; start at different ages, attend as they wish, and mature at their own rate.) When the leaders of the different ages, including adults, have an intentional plan to help people progress not only according to age, but to faith development, the disciple-making process is more fruitful.

Families: The parents, guardians, or other family members of the students will want to know what the plan is for their children, youth, or themselves, and they will definitely want to know what is going on in the classes and groups their children attend. As you keep them informed, you may also find among them prayer partners, substitute teachers or nursery helpers, chaperones, and future teachers.

The pastoral leader: When the pastoral leader is the only staff person, you will want to work closely with the pastor to ensure that what happens in the church school and other education/formation experiences supports and is supported by the worship ministry (and evangelism, missions, and so on). In smaller churches, the pastor may be the only person with a theological education. He or she can be a great partner in helping to identify the theological direction of various curricula, which is particularly important if you deviate from United Methodist curriculum resources. The pastor may also provide some basic Bible instruction to the teachers.

Staff related to Christian education: If there is a staff person (paid or volunteer) who works in Christian education, discipleship, program, or one or more age-levels, he or she may be expected to work in partnership with you. In addition, this staff person may have primary responsibility for visioning and planning for Christian education. Be clear that you wish to be a partner.

SECONDARY PARTNERS

The church council: You are a member of the council and together, the council members will engage with the pastor and other staff (if any) in the visioning, planning, and implementation of all the church's ministries. Your role will be to ensure that the ministry of Christian education and formation is a vital part of the entire disciple making process in your church.

Other church leaders, according to function: Become familiar with the responsibilities of the other leaders with whom you will work, on occasion. If there is an issue related to maintenance, equipment, or building codes, for example, you will take it to the **trustees.** When you work on devising and maintaining a budget, you will do so in conjunction with the **finance committee** or the **treasurer.** If the church school wants to offer a special emphasis or presentation in worship, you will discuss those plans with the **pastor** and/or **worship committee.** When gathering people to form your Christian education team (if you do that yourself), you may ask for assistance from the **committee on nominations.**

It is generally wise to think holistically so that when you embark on a course of action, you consult with or inform others who may have a stake in those plans or who will be affected by them. People are much more supportive when they are not surprised or excluded inappropriately.

Start with the Current Ministry

You have a description of your responsibilities (or will get one) and you know the key relationships. Before plunging into a "Do List," take a good look at what is already happening and how it happens. Having a handle on the current reality will give you an idea of where the needs are, what the strengths are, what your assets are, and what you have on hand to enable this ministry to go forward. Discover

- What classes are in place? What ages are covered?
- Who are all the teachers, substitutes, and group leaders? Where is their contact information kept?
- What events or special happenings are being planned and who is planning them?
- Where are all the supplies and equipment stored? Who keeps track of them?

- How do decisions get made? Are there stakeholders who are not "official" decision makers, but whose opinions are sought?
- What policies and procedures do you need to know? (For example, the Safe Sanctuaries® policies, how things get ordered and paid for, what is done in case of fire or other emergency, what is supposed to happen if a minor is sick or injured).
- What is your budget and what is included in it?
- Is there any important history you should know? (Before discarding that dilapidated rocker in the nursery, find out if it was a memorial gift!)

Teachers and Team Members

You may already have an education team in place—or age-level councils or some other sub-group related to Christian education and formation. If you are in a large or mid-sized church, the committee on nominations and leader development may recruit your entire team. However, in many cases, you will have to pull together this team yourself.

Forming a Team

One typical way to form a team is to recruit people we know and/or who have a passion for the work that the team is to do. That certainly makes some sense. What can happen, though, is that there are particular functions needed to implement the strategies of the team but no one on the team with those skills. The other side of that formation picture, then, is to think through the specific kinds of skills or gifts needed and then recruit people who possess them.

Most likely, you will work from the mid-point. Your ministry team may be constituted in part by people who are there by virtue of their own leadership role, such as a church school superintendant, curriculum secretary, or staff person. Even if your entire team is "inherited," you may be able to expand where you need to in order to have the resident skills required.

There is a certain "chicken and egg" process in forming a team with the particular skill set. The team does the visioning and planning, but until the planning is done, you may not have identified all the skills needed on the team. So, start with what you know: the details of the current ministry.

As you take a closer look at everything already in place, you can back up a step to envision what it takes to implement those plans. Video presentation coming up in worship? Your team may need someone who is tech-savvy. Planning for a community-wide vacation Bible school? Your team will definitely need someone who is a good manager and handles detail well. Having a church school-sponsored breakfast each week for the community's needy children? Your team may require someone who knows how to organize and prepare food for a crowd. When you and your existing team members have some clarity about your goals (or hopes and dreams) you will identify the skills and gifts resident on the team already and then can work to expand as needed. The pastoral leader and committee on nominations may be able to suggest people. If the church keeps an up-to-date file from "gifts and talents" surveys, that would be a good place to start.

TIP: *You can always form a short-term project team for the occasional activities that require special skills. You don't have to have every possible gift represented on the team at all times.*

Care and Nurture of Teachers

Your teachers are the greatest asset—other than the Trinity—that your ministry area will have. Research has shown that the teacher is seven times more important than the curriculum, or anything else. An excellent teacher can pick up the poorest piece of curriculum and make a go of it, but excellent curriculum in the hands of a poor teacher will seldom, if ever, carry a successful class alone.

RECRUITING

In informal surveys, groups of teachers and other education leaders have been asked to jot down the words or phrases that have been used to recruit them. Typical responses included "We need you"; "It's easy and won't take much time"; "We'll help you"; "You'll be good at it"; "The kids asked for you"; even, "I'm dying, and I need you to take my place." (Honest!) Then, the group was asked to note words and phrases that identified themselves as teachers or leaders. Those typical responses included "Gifted"; "Sharing my own learning"; "Mentor or guide"; "Compassionate"; "Nurturer."

To be fair, the first set of answers also included remarks like "You have a great gift" or "You are wonderful with children." And the second set of responses added "Inadequate" or "Insecure." Nevertheless, what was most characteristic of the recruitment statements was that they were dismissive, desperate, or deceptive. The self assessments, on the other hand, generally found the teachers to feel valuable, valued, and passionate about sharing their knowledge and nurturing those in their charge. This must be evidence of the power of the Holy Spirit, because it is almost inconceivable that desperate recruiting techniques alone would produce dedicated and skilled teachers.

When you recruit teachers and substitutes, keep these points in mind.
- **Be honest!** Asking a gifted and busy person to do something and then hiding, distorting, or "dumbing down" the details is unfair and insulting. Know what the obligations are and state them honestly. If you aren't sure about something, confess and find out.

- **Call forth specific gifts.** People say yes when they will get what they need, but also when they have something to offer. Not everyone is aware of their own gifts, and knowing that someone else has seen them is powerful.

- **Communicate expectations clearly.** Know what you want to happen both in the classroom and outside. Don't be afraid to set high expectations. It is not enough that a teacher shows up on time, prepared. Indicate what character traits you're looking for and what behaviors you expect. *Provide a job description in writing.* Tell them about policies or procedures that will affect them (such as the need for a background check).

- **Have a plan for the teacher's continuing spiritual and biblical development.** This should be in place or clearly in the plans before teachers are recruited. If this is a condition of teaching, say so. In any case, you will want someone who is mature and secure in their faith, adaptable, a capable listener, open-minded, and light-hearted.

- **Set boundaries.** Know also what is beyond your request; what the teacher will not have to do, such as teaching through the year, but not for vacation Bible school or not having to pay for their own supplies. Be clear about the lines of accountability.

- **Ask for the teacher to enter into a covenant,** including signing a covenant agreemer   Just as you benefit from having a job description, you can have som .ning in writing for the teachers, which they may sign. While you .ay not desire such formality, having this level of agreement and   arity helps if one or the other fails to keep the covenant and when it is time for evaluation.

- **Give the potential teacher time to think and pray.** It's better not to press for an instant answer, which also means that you shouldn't be asking at the 11th hour. If you're told no, you may respectfully ask for the reason why and work to remedy it, but be graceful about rejection. Keep the door open for another request at a better time.

- **Be personal and specific.** Begging from the pulpit often yields nothing or something you don't want. It is better not to have that 6th grade class than to have an unsuitable teacher there. The congregation may be unhappy with that, but they need to know that a "warm body" is not enough and that the education leaders are serious about the value of this ministry. Call and/or visit the people you want to recruit and follow up that conversation with either another conversation or a note.

- **Consider having a pair of teachers in each group or a teacher and helper.** Two responsible people in the class relieves the load on a solo teacher, provides for coverage in the class if one teacher is absent or has to leave, and increases the creative teaching possibilities.

CARING FOR AND ABOUT TEACHERS

Your teachers almost certainly give their time freely, so the first word is *Grace*! This does not mean that you are stuck putting up with things that are unacceptable. It is reasonable to assume that the teachers want and try to do well, so grace and patience are the first priority.

While there will always be high-maintenance volunteers who require a lot of attention, many will be just fine with a few thoughtful gestures like these.

- **Be grateful and complimentary.** When there is an honest good word to share, share it. Affirm what the teachers do and who they are.

- **Be aware, with proper discretion, of what is going on in their lives.** Adjust accordingly when a teacher hits a rough spot and be attentive to the kind of support the teacher needs.

- **Offer to help or to smooth the way when you can, and then be sure to do it.** As the leader, one principle responsibility is to help ensure that others can do what they were asked to do. If there are conditions of their teaching, such as a requirement for continuing education, see that it can happen. When supplies and/or equipment are needed, see that they are on hand or work with the teacher on how to accommodate requests that can't be fulfilled.

- **Host a beginning-of-year orientation,** especially for newcomers, to acquaint them with policies, curriculum, the supply closet, and so on.

- **Ask the teachers** how they are doing, what they need, and what feedback they have to improve the education ministry. Take it seriously; they are the ones in the "trenches" each week to see how and what is happening (or not). This is one way to value their insight.

- **Be sure the rest of the church, and the pastor, knows and appreciates the service and ministry the teachers render.** An annual service of consecration or a celebratory banquet for the teachers helps to elevate the importance of the teaching office. Short articles on your church's website or in the newsletter highlight this ministry and attract support.

- **Have a stable of substitutes and keep them trained along with the regular teachers.** Be sure everyone knows the procedures to arrange for a substitute and how to get in touch with them.

Planning

Often one of the first steps in planning is to ask, "What should we do?" This is an important question, but not the first question. A prior question is, "What do we want to accomplish?" To answer that, we need to have a vision of that accomplishment, then the mission describing what our essential tasks are.

Mission and Vision

A vision is a portrait of what your goal will look like when it is accomplished. While disciple-making is never fully accomplished, we must have some idea of what that disciple looks like to know if we have "made one." So, if the church's **mission** is to make disciples of Jesus Christ for the transformation of the world, the **vision** is "disciples are..." followed by a description of the characteristics and behaviors of disciples who fulfill ministry in your setting.

Your church may have its own vision statement, and if so, work with that one. You may want to have a different vision statement that is more specific to Christian education, yet supports the church's vision.

For example, your church is in an urban setting. "The **mission** of the Christian education ministry at First UMC Downtown is to form, educate, and nurture disciples of Jesus Christ. Our **vision** is disciples who are grounded in Scripture, steeped in love for the 'least of these,' and engaged in life-giving service in the name of Christ." **Mission** is the big picture of what you do; **vision** is the big picture of what it looks like when you have succeeded.

Once you have clarity on what your mission and vision are, then you can begin to plan the goals and strategies, which are smaller, more specific pictures of the interim steps that cumulatively lead to the big picture. So, what would need to happen at First UMC Downtown to fulfill that mission and vision? Three goals are implied in the vision. People who are
- grounded in Scripture
- steeped in love for the 'least of these'
- engaged in life-giving service

The strategies by which you will implement the goals might include:
- basic Bible study opportunities for all ages
- mid-week DISCIPLE groups for adults
- coordinated worship and study opportunities that center on parables of the Kingdom

- thematic studies that combine learning about and practicing the spiritual disciplines, particularly prayer and justice
- coordinated work with the missions committee for service/mission opportunities in the community and beyond.

Guard against the temptation to have only short-term, easily reachable goals. You do need early successes. They breed further success, and those "victories" are life-giving and motivating. That is what keeps you going while you tackle the more ambitious, longer-term goals that may feel daunting or elusive at the first step. First UMC Downtown, for example, may start with a VBS just for their own church this summer, but a longer-term goal may be to have THE community VBS that not only gathers in the kids who are normally overlooked, but that also offers courses for parents that will help them up and out of poor or modest circumstances.

MAKING YOUR VISION AND MISSION "STICK"

The importance of keeping your team focused, motivated, and faithful cannot be overstated. To do that, you must have the vision and mission "stick." Your team and the congregation have to remember what they claim they want to do and why they want to do it. As a leader, a vital part of your work is to make the vision "stick." Why doesn't it stick?

- **Too much success** (!) can lead to too many options and ideas. If they are not carefully vetted through the mission/vision, you run the risk of being too diffuse and losing focus.
- **Too much failure** is discouraging. We also tend to blame the idea rather than the strategy. If something doesn't work, examine why. The idea may be an excellent one, but the way to get at it needs to be revised.
- **Everything in between.** Life intervenes, plans change, people come and go, leadership shifts, a problem arises, things just happen. This may be the most difficult reason because it requires constant vigilance. All the little bits and pieces that distract us are often innocent enough by themselves, but the cumulative effect can be quite disruptive.

How can you keep your team and congregation focused on the vision?

- **Talk about the vision** in strategic ways. Remind the team, tell stories of your dreams, define what you want to do, and be consistent.
- **Celebrate the successes** and be deliberate about looking for the bright spots and learning in what is regarded as a failure. Something in that failure will help you learn how to get where you want to go. Avoid downward spiral thinking.
- **Live it out.** Be an example of what you want to accomplish and look for all the partners you can find, even if they aren't on the team.

Set Priorities

It is important in your planning to use **the vision and mission as filters** for the ideas you develop. Many of the plans conceived by your team will be excellent ideas, but you can't do everything. The way you choose is to hold up the idea against the vision and mission. If the idea, no matter how wonderful, does not lead to the end you have envisioned, you should think carefully about whether to do it.

Capacity is another element in prioritizing. Do you have enough people, time, money, skill, motivation, space, equipment, and supplies to do what you want? Guard against "scarcity thinking," though. Do not focus on what you do not have; rather, look broadly for all the assets available, both now and later with some planning and careful work.

Jesus told his followers that he came so that they and we would have an abundant life, and we do. But we forget sometimes. Even a tiny congregation with a very modest budget has some space and some people who have gifts. What are those gifts? Start with that and then think prayerfully about how gifts and vision combine for ministry.

Develop short- and longer-term goals and strategies. Plan for immediate successes as a way to encourage your team to work on longer-term plans. When long-terms plans are conceived, it may be helpful to target a completion or launch date, then work backward. If we are to develop THE community VBS within five years, what specifically has to be done by the fourth year, the third, and so on back to the present? Once those interim targets are set, you can determine if you have the capacity to meet each one (all other things being equal) or if you need to push the target farther out. This allows for strategic thinking and planning so that all the foundational steps are in place.

KEEP A CALENDAR

One tool that may help to keep you on target is a deadline calendar. Your long-range planning tells you what has to be done by next year, but if it isn't on the calendar, with the interim steps needed to do everything, plans can be backed up indefinitely because steps didn't get started or completed on time.

In addition to a deadline calendar, be sure to coordinate your plans and activities with the church calendar. All the ministry groups are making plans and setting dates, so be sure you are working together not competing.

Leading Meetings

Meetings can be exciting, stimulating, motivating, and productive—or they can be a deadly waste of time. Your task as leader is to be sure that when you do gather your team, the endeavor will be worth the time and energy. *A good meeting actually saves time,* so plan well. How to do that?

Know what kind of meeting you want to have, and stick to it. It may be more efficient and productive to have a single purpose, such as planning, report/update/problem solving, or visioning, rather than trying to do all of that in the same meeting. Such a diffuse approach asks your members to change mental gears too often.

For an initial meeting of a new team, you may want to spend the first gathering getting to know one another, hearing your dreams and hopes, exploring your gifts and passions, and just reviewing (not evaluating) the "what is" of the current ministry. Subsequent meetings may spend some time evaluating what is going on in light of the current mission and vision statements, if you have them. If not, visioning, or asking several "what if" questions, would be in order. The next step would be to examine how the current plans help to achieve the vision, then to identify any big gaps. That is where the planning process may develop.

Consider these tips in leading successful meetings.
- Get the date on the church calendar and notify everyone; inform group members ahead of time so that they can prepare.
- Have an agenda; know what you want to accomplish.
- Start with prayer or other spiritual practice to center the team and start on time.
- Stick to the theme: visioning, or planning, or group building, and so on.
- Keep the vision in mind; make it "stick."
- Lead and monitor so that everyone has a chance to participate and so that multiple viewpoints are heard. Interrupt or gracefully redirect group members who dominate, manipulate, or sidetrack.
- Keep on track; allow people to talk, even digress a bit, but be sure to pull back to the task at hand before people get lost in some bunny trail.
- Be sensitive to when to direct and when to ask questions.
- Restate decisions clearly and be sure they are recorded.
- Share responsibility for who does what; allow members their proper ownership of the ministry and its tasks.
- Be clear about who is to do what and by when and make note of it. If a report is required, identify what is needed and when.
- Check in between meetings to see that work is progressing.

Evaluation and Measurement

You, your team, and your church want to have a vital ministry. Periodic evaluation with established measures allows you to avoid the twin dangers of 1) continuous doing without evaluating and 2) evaluating simply by way of numbers. One way to guard against the "we've always done it that way" syndrome is to build into plans when and how you will evaluate and the measures by which you will judge your efforts.

The evaluation process brings together your vision and mission, the goals and strategies used to bring that vision to fruition, and the measures by which you compare your results with your desired outcomes. Other terms gaining popularity that deal with measures are "metrics" or "dashboard" (like your car's at-a-glance panel of indicators). For more in-depth help see *Measures Evaluation Tool* at www.umvitalcongregations.com in the Setting Goals tab.

What Are Measures?

Measures are indicators of activity and impact, and they are implied by both the mission and vision statements and your established goals and strategies. Let's return to our example of First UMC Downtown. The chart on page 25 will give you a visual example of possible measures.

In this case, the desired outcomes (the vision) are for "disciples who are grounded in Scripture, steeped in love for the 'least of these,' and engaged in life-giving service in the name of Christ." The flow of activity that leads to that vision (your mission statement) is first to form, then educate, then nurture. It's helpful to define what you mean by each of these indicators. If there is no clarity about what you meant, exactly, you can have numerous subjective opinions about whether you did what you intended to do.

The flow of the ministry, stated in the mission, should have definitions and outcomes (in the vision) that match up and make sense. The example provides a definition and outcome, along with possible strategies and measures to evaluate it. Measures should be **quantitative** and **qualitative** (read on).

This exercise may "squeeze the brain" a bit, especially since it is so easy to describe strategies instead of results or definitions. Intentionally developing strategies and the measures that evaluate them will strengthen your ministry, and ultimately, it is a blessing to the teachers and participants. This is why.
- Having a plan gives focus and direction. It helps to see where there are gaps and needs in a holistic educational ministry.
- Teachers who know what is expected and how you will evaluate can be more confident that their teaching aligns with the plan.

• If problems arise or if the teachers need more training, there is a way to talk about it and deal with it.

• A plan with specific strategies and measures will have been approved by the education committee and, ideally, by the church council. **When the people executing the plan do as well as they can what everyone agreed upon, and the plan doesn't work so well, examine the strategies rather than criticizing the volunteers who are doing their best.** Teachers are nurtured better when they know they will be supported during a "failure," especially when the strategy is flawed.

QUALITATIVE VS. QUANTITATIVE

Quantitative measures are the easiest to define because they can be counted: 100 people attended Bible study or there was a 22 percent increase in giving to the Sunday school service project. These measures serve a purpose, especially if numbers that we want to go up are going down. That at least indicates that something might be wrong, though it doesn't tell us what.

Neither do numbers tell us what is actually happening to the 100 people who attended that Bible study and that is really what we need to know. Are those participants being formed in Christian values or are they spending most of the time socializing? When "growth in Christian discipleship" is the goal, the measures have to identify changes in character, spiritual maturity, knowledge of the faith, and shifts of behavior. Knowledge and behavior are more "testable" and observable, yet there are ways to recognize qualitative differences. One basic faith and discipleship question—"Am I more loving than I was a year ago?"— gives rise to other evaluative questions. If I am more loving, how do I know and how do I show it? Consider these measures and indicators of spiritual growth (in no particular order). How many others can you describe?

1. Regular participation in worship
2. Personal stories attesting to spiritual growth and change
3. Eliminates "ungodly" behaviors (or works diligently toward that goal)
4. Greater financial investment in ministry
5. Invests in ministry and nurture of children and youth
6. Intentionally teaches/models Christian practices within the family
7. Habituated in one or more means of grace
8. Seeks continuing education and formation activities
9. Understands and lives out baptismal vows
10. Greater evidence of the "fruits of the Spirit"
11. Demonstrates mindfulness in listening to God and seeking God's direction
12. Engages in works of mercy (service) and works for justice

SAMPLE: Flow and Measures Grid for Christian Education at First UMC Downtown

FORM	EDUCATE	NURTURE
DEFINITIONS: Shape congregational members of all ages in Christian values	Teach the Scriptures—what they mean, and how they are applied—and the heritage of witness and service of the Church	Care for congregational members and model discipleship in the form of outreach, witness, and service
RESULTS: Persons have values of love, justice, and service in a congregation that cares for them	Persons know the content and meaning of Scriptures, of the heritage of the UMC, and the missions of the Church	Persons mature in faith, take responsibility for living as disciples, and serve and mentor others
STRATEGIES: **F1.** Place Sunday school teachers in covenant groups for personal spiritual growth. **F2.** Lead study of *A Plain Account of Christian Perfection*	**E1.** Provide study classes for all ages **E2.** Train teachers using the basic material from "What Every Teacher Needs to Know"	**N1.** Train 12 persons as mentors for confirmation class and 15 for new member class members **N2.** Plan Bible study for and partner with missions committee for winter dinner/shelter ministry
MEASURES: **F1a.** 70% of teachers engaged in covenant group **F1b.** 70% of those teachers report increase in and satisfaction with personal spiritual disciplines **F1c.** 50% of teachers emphasizing Christian values in their class	**E2a.** 50% of current teachers and 80% of new teachers participate in training **E2b.** 75% of trained teachers demonstrate greater mastery in teaching **E2c.** 80% of teachers improve self-test scores in the training inventory	**N1a.** All confirmation students and new members partnered with mentor **N1b.** 75% of mentored persons report greater sense of belonging and personal care from the relationship **N1c.** 40% of confirmands and new members engaged in shelter ministry share their faith with shelter guests

Evaluating Ministry

Who evaluates depends in part on *what* is evaluated. Your education team, possibly with the church council, will assess the major strategies and goals you developed against the measures you established. An annual review of the overall plan should suffice, though it is helpful to conduct interim evaluations of specific parts of the plan. Waiting until the end of the year for feedback on the summer program will lose a lot of detail; too much time has passed.

This is what your team will want to evaluate.

* **The function of the team itself.** Is there a balance of gifts against the needs and skills among team members so that the ministry is accomplished? Are the meetings productive and satisfying? Are members following through well with what they have agreed to do? What additions or changes would be helpful?
* **The long- and short-term plans.** Are you meeting your short-term goals? Are the interim steps of the longer-range plan being accomplished? What problems or barriers have been overcome and what remains? Who is designated to work at what? Is that happening? How well? Are the plans accomplishing your vision? How can you tell?
* **The specific strategies, against your measures,** as described earlier.
* **The teachers and group leaders, by themselves.** Providing a structure for self-reflection will help them identify accomplishments, strengths, needs for training or nurture, and so on.
* **The teachers and group leaders, by others.** Those others might be you and/or the team, the group members, parents (for children's classes or groups), or some combination. Again, when teachers know the expectations and measures, there should be few surprises, particularly if they have been asked to do some self-assessment first.

DEALING WITH POOR OUTCOMES

Seldom will everything run smoothly with exactly the right people who possess exactly the right gifts. If you are not getting the results you want, first determine if the strategies are ineffective or have not had time to work. Regroup there, as necessary.

If the issue is personnel, the person in question may realize this first after self-assessment. Other persons may not realize the need or desire a change that must be made. Express appreciation and honor the contribution, but work together to find out where those gifts are a better fit. Enlisting the support of the pastor or someone trusted by the person may be a benefit. Always strive for a win-win situation; this isn't a contest and shouldn't be a battle of wills.

Administration

the nitty gritty details of Christian education may be either the most-
or the least-liked aspects of this ministry. Administration is a spiritual
gift and a much-needed service, even if it feels like a necessary evil.
Your responsibility is to see that these things are done, though some or all
of it may be delegated to a team member who is good with detail work.

With your ministry team, review the purpose of your educational ministries as you have come to understand it through study, conversation,
and prayer. Identify the biblical and theological foundations that undergird
your purpose. Restate what values, attitudes, behavior, knowledge, and
skills you hope people will develop through participating in your congregation's ministry of Christian education.

"Admin 101"

Some administrative tasks come up routinely. Most likely, you are not the
only one with responsibility here, so find out the practice at your church.

RECORD KEEPING

- The average number of people attending church school, small groups,
  mid-week classes/programs (for Charge Conference information). You
  may record attendance, at least numbers, if not names.
- Health or information forms for minor children and vulnerable adults.
- Permission slips for any off-campus activities.
- Roster of teachers and substitutes with contact information, perhaps with
  birthdays or other special days to remember through the year.
- Regularly used supplies.
- List of vendors/stores whose services you use or who carry the supplies
  you need for your ministry, and the church's tax ID number.
- Who has keys to what locks.

POLICIES AND PROCEDURES

A **policy** describes **what is to be done** or **what must be done** (and perhaps
why). Policies are directive; often instituted because of legal obligations,
insurance requirements, safety reasons, or moral imperatives. A *procedure*
describes **how something is to happen,** whether it is a policy or not. As
you get acquainted with this ministry, pay attention to how things get done.

Find out what policies are in place already, if they are actually written
down, and who the "custodian" of the policy is. (If there isn't much in writing, encourage this.) Trustees, for example, are responsible initially for

bequests or material donations, by provision of the *Discipline*. If a donor offers a new swing set for the playground, you must refer that gift to the trustees.

The unique setting of your congregation may require unique policies. Typically, churches have policies (or procedures) that relate to:

Safety
- A *Safe Sanctuaries®* policy (see Resources) for the well-being of minors and vulnerable adults, as well as for protection of the church and its members from liability
- For the use of playground or other equipment that is accessible on church property
- For health, first aid, or emergency situations
- Who is allowed to have keys and for how long

Vehicles
- Drivers license/driving record requirements for use of church-owned buses, vans, or other vehicles
- Use of private vehicles for church-related events
- Age of drivers
- Ratio of adults to minors traveling in any vehicles

Use of equipment, supplies, or space
- Who is authorized to run equipment
- Who purchases new equipment or supplies, how much they are authorized to spend, and with whom can you do business
- Who decides how space is shared, who gets to store what and where

Spending money (see the next section)

Budgeting

You may have nothing more to do with the budget than submitting an annual request to the finance committee, but you are encouraged to be proactive about budgeting for your ministry area. Start with what you are already doing. Check with the church treasurer or finance chairperson to see the plan for the coming year. If there is a lump sum listed in the budget, find out what is included in it. Most churches will have a unified budget, meaning there is only one. If your church takes an offering in the church school that is held in a separate budget for Christian education, learn how that process works and whether that is the only source of income to finance education needs. You may also take up an offering on Christian Education Sunday, though most, if not all, will go to the annual conference to administer. See Resources for a link to more information about budgeting.

A typical budget detail may include:
- curriculum resources, Bibles for third graders, and/or books for the church library
- supplies—paper, art supplies, scissors, nursery items (like disposable diapers and wipes)
- equipment and supplies (DVD players, DVDs or CDs, batteries, video equipment, media carts, extension cords), replacement costs
- promotion and celebration (advertising, gifts for teacher appreciation)
- travel/transportation (field trips, busing for neighborhood children)
- training (educational/development events for teachers)

If you are to keep track of expenditures and needs, ask the treasurer for any forms (like check requests or requisition forms) that are used. You may recruit someone for your team who is good with budget and finance.

Some teachers are accustomed to paying for their own supplies, curriculum, or more. While this generosity is to be celebrated, a few caveats are in order.
- First, **teachers should not be expected to bear these expenses.** If this ministry is valued, that should be reflected in the church budget.

- Second, if teachers **are** expected to pay out-of-pocket expenses, they must know when they are asked to teach what a likely contribution is.

- Third, if teachers **do** offer these gifts, keep a record of what they spend. This can be done anonymously, but the church still must know the actual costs of this ministry so that the budget will accommodate it or will work toward it. Find ways to express appreciation.

Curriculum

"Curriculum" actually refers to the entire educational plan. "Curriculum resources" are the books, leaflets, DVDs, and such that are tools for teaching and learning. At the least, you and/or your committee may have responsibility for selecting and purchasing curriculum resources. Adult classes are usually free to obtain their own, and often do, but particular care is necessary for resources for children and youth.

The *Book of Discipline* requires that The United Methodist Church provide curriculum resources that are sound educationally and appropriate within the bounds of United Methodist theology. By extension, **it is expected that United Methodist congregations will use those resources**. You will find them in the *Forecast* catalog. Official United Methodist resources are identified in *Forecast* with the ⳩RC icon.

Check Resources for more information on selecting curriculum, getting catalogs, and using the advisors at Curric-U-Phone. If you select and order curriculum resources, keep these things in mind:

- **The theological slant:** Is it United Methodist or compatible?
- **Age-level appropriateness:** Can students do what is suggested and understand what is said?
- **Inclusive:** Are people of various ethnic or ability groups represented and presented positively in images, stories, and cultural assumptions?
- **Ease of use:** Is the skill level of the teacher sufficient for what the lessons require? Is the material too simple? Does the material require equipment or supplies that are readily available?

Promotion

Keep the ministry of Christian education and formation in the front of the congregation's mind. Communicating with the congregation has several purposes. It celebrates the teachers, students, and life-long learning. It supports and focuses on the church's vision and mission. It encourages participation and lifts up the needs of the ministry. It offers a place for everyone to reflect on the Bible, share thoughts and experiences with others, and make meaning of what they encounter and do in life.

You are limited only by your imagination; here are a few ideas on promotion to get you started.

- Recruit greeters or hosts to direct people to the correct class or group.
- Put a brief report, spot advertisement, or highlight in the various church communications—bulletin, website, newsletter, email, etc.
- Use indoor and outdoor bulletin boards, signs, banners, or posters, especially for occasional or seasonal offerings for the whole church and/or community.
- Use conference communications, website, UM Reporter, and so on.
- Encourage the congregation, teachers, and class/group participants to talk up what they do with others and to invite others.

IN CONCLUSION

A ministry of Christian education and formation requires attention to numerous details, planning for classes and events, ordering supplies and curriculum, dealing with classroom dynamics, equipping teachers, and much more. At the heart of it is the desire to serve God in the task of disciple-making. Forming and transforming a people who know, love, and serve God is the ultimate goal. What call and privilege could be more important than that?

Resources

** Denotes our top picks. (See also www.gbod.org/education and a listing of article links on the CD included in the Guidelines set.)

LEADERSHIP
**Christian Educators Fellowship (www.cefumc.org) is a professional national organization for leaders in Christian education and formation. Many annual conferences have a chapter.

**Foundations.* Provides guidelines for education in The United Methodist Church, found at www.gbod.org/education.

**Guidelines for Leading Your Congregation: *Adult Ministries, Youth Ministries, Children's Ministries, Family Ministries* (Nashville: Cokesbury, 2012.)

Making Vision Stick, by Andy Stanley. Available in MP3 or print (check Google). Some material for page 20 provided by this download.

The Nuts and Bolts of Christian Education, by Delia Halverson (Nashville: Abingdon Press, 2000. ISBN 978-068707-116-6).

Safe Sanctuaries: The Church Responds to Abuse, Neglect, and Exploitation of Older Adults, by Joy Thornburg Melton (Nashville: Discipleship Resources, 2012. ISBN 978-0-88177-613-3).

***Safe Sanctuaries: Reducing the Risk of Abuse in the Church for Children and Youth*, by Joy Thornburg Melton (Nashville: Discipleship Resources, 2008. ISBN 978-0-88177-543-3). Spanish, ISBN 978-0-88177-402-3.

Teaching Today's Teachers to Teach, revised edition, by Donald L. Griggs (Nashville: Abingdon Press, 2003. ISBN 978-068704-954-7).

TEACHING AND LEARNING
Christian Education in the Small Membership Church, by Karen Tye (Nashville: Abingdon Press, 2008. ISBN 978-068765-099-6).

The Church as Learning Community: A Comprehensive Guide to Christian Education, by Norma Cook Everist (Nashville: Abingdon Press, 2002. ISBN 978-0-687-04500-6).

Formation in Faith: The Congregational Ministry of Making Disciples, by Sondra Mattaei (Nashville: Abingdon Press, 2008. ISBN 978-068764-973-0).

**iTeach*: monthly e-letter for teachers; www.gbod.org/education.

Our Spiritual Brain: Integrating Brain Research and Faith Development, by Barbara Bruce (Nashville: Abingdon Press, 2002. ISBN 978-0-687-09266-6). *Raising Children to Love Their Neighbors: Practical Resources for Congregations*, by Carolyn Brown (Nashville: Abingdon Press, 2008. ISBN 978-068765-142-9).

Soul Stories: African American Christian Education, Revised Edition, by Anne E. Streaty Wimberly (Nashville: Abingdon Press, 2005. ISBN 978-068749-432-3).

Triangular Teaching: A New Way of Teaching the Bible to Adults, by Barbara Bruce (Nashville: Abingdon Press, 2007. ISBN 978-068764-352-3).

WEB RESOURCES
Look for these articles at www.gbod.org/education.

- Assess Your Congregation's Policies
- Assess Your Facilities and Equipment
- Assessing Ministry
- Budgeting for Christian Education
- Choosing Curriculum Resources
- Comprehensive Plan
- Creating Job Descriptions
- Development Through the Life Span
- Evaluating Your Ministry
- Forming an Effective Christian Education Team
- Getting the Word Out
- Meetings That Nurture Christian Education
- Planning for Christian Education
- Recruiting . . . Teachers
- What Every Teacher Needs to Know

Effective Teaching for Transformation: a series of six ready-to-go 3-hour workshops, plus a demonstration workshop that blends elements of all six to give a preview of the series. (www.gbod.org/education; in the DIY tab)

Local Church Discipler/Educator self-guided study resource: a series of six modules that are self-guided outlines for professional development for staff who are hired locally or from within their church to serve their church in some area related to Christian education, formation, and discipleship. (www.gbod.org/education; in the DIY tab)

Helps for Planning, Evaluating, and Measuring your ministry efforts: www.umvitalcongregations.com; includes assistance for the metrics required by your annual conference. See also similar information on the Guidelines CD.

1-800-972-0433 (item # M184) or downloaded from www.gbod.org/laity; items below marked with **LL** are in the Learning and Leading series and can be found in the LMER catalog.

Mainline or Methodist? Rediscovering Our Evangelistic Mission, by Scott Kisker (Nashville: Discipleship Resources, 2008. ISBN 978-0-88177-541-9).

Missional: Joining God in the Neighborhood, by Alan J. Roxburgh (Grand Rapids, Baker Books, 2011. ISBN 978-0-8010-7231-4).

Re-Jesus: A Wild Messiah for a Missional Church, by Michael Frost and Alan Hirsch (Peabody: Hendrikson Publishers, 2009. ISBN 978-159-856-228-6).

The United Methodist Way: Living Our Beliefs, by Kenneth L. Carder (Nashville: Discipleship Resources, 2009. ISBN 978-0-88177-571-6).

What Every Leader Needs to Know (series). (Nashville: Discipleship Resources, 2010). Order PDFs from www.upperroom.org/bookstore.

SPIRITUAL GIFTS AND SPIRITUAL DISCIPLINES
Accountable Discipleship: Living in God's Household, by Steven W. Manskar (Nashville: Discipleship Resources, 2000. ISBN 978-0-881-77-339-2). **LL**

Class Leaders; Recovering a Tradition, by David Lowes Watson (Eugene: Wipf and Stock, 2002. ISBN: 978-1-57910-954-7. **LL**

Devotional Life in the Wesleyan Tradition, by Steve Harper (Nashville: Upper Room Books, 1995. ISBN 978-0-835-8-0740-1). **LL**

Each One a Minister, by William J. Carter (Nashville: Discipleship Resources, 2007. ISBN 978-0-881-77-375-0). **LL**

Eight Life-Enriching Practices of United Methodists, by Henry H. Knight III (Nashville: Abingdon Press, 2001. ISBN 978-0-687-08734-1).

Opening Ourselves to Grace; Basic Christian Practices, Produced by Mark Purushotham (DVD available from Discipleship Resources, 2007. ISBN 978-0-881-77-508-2).

Restoring the Wesleyan Class Meeting, by Dr. James B. Scott and Dr. Molly Davis Scott (Dallas: Provident Publishing, 2008. ISBN 978-0-97786-732-5). (This may be available only through Cokesbury.)

This Holy Mystery: A United Methodist Understanding of Holy Communion, by Gayle Carlton Felton (Nashville: Discipleship Resources, 2005. ISBN 978-0-881-77-457-3).

www.gbod.org/smallgroup/cd

CHRISTIAN CONFERENCING
Concepts in Leadership I and II, by Brian Jackson and Sandy Zeigler, (**LL** download) from www.upperroom.org/bookstore, DRPDF7 and DRPDF13.

Leading in Prayer*, by Mary O. Benedict (Nashville: Discipleship Resources, 2007. ISBN: 978-0-88177-492-4 OR Revised edition by Betsey Heavner. Download from www.upperroom.org/bookstore, DRPDF437). **LL

CHANGE/CONFLICT
Appreciative Inquiry Handbook: For Leaders of Change, by David Cooperrider (San Francisco: Berrett-Koehler Publishers, Inc., 2008. ISBN 978-1-576-75-493-1).

**Inclusion: Making Room for Grace*, by Eric H.F. Law (St. Louis: Chalice Press, 2000. ISBN 978-0-827-2-1620-4).

The Power of Appreciative Inquiry, by Diana Whitney and Amanda Trosten-Bloom (San Francisco: Berrett-Koehler Publishers, Inc. 2003. ISBN 978-1-605-09-3284).

Sacred Acts, Holy Change: Faithful Diversity and Practical Transformation, by Eric H.F. Law (St. Louis: Chalice Press, 2002. ISBN 978-0-827-234-52-9).

**Switch: How to Change Things When Change Is Hard*, by Chip Heath & Dan Heath (New York: Broadway Books, 2010) ISBN 978-0-385-52875-7).

**The Thin Book of Appreciative Inquiry*, by Sue Annis Hammond (Thin Book Publishing Co. 1998. ISBN 978-0-966-5373-1-49).

www.justpeaceumc.org